Nelson Mandela

Jayne Woodhouse

First published in Great Britain by Heinemann Library
Halley Court, Jordan Hill, Oxford OX2 8EJ,
a division of Reed Educational and Professional Publishing Ltd.
Heinemann is a registered trademark of Reed Educational & Professional Publishing Limited.

OXFORD FLORENCE PRAGUE MADRID ATHENS
MELBOURNE AUCKLAND KUALA LUMPUR SINGAPORE TOKYO
IBADAN NAIROBI KAMPALA JOHANNESBURG GABORONE
PORTSMOUTH NH (USA) CHICAGO MEXICO CITY SAO PAULO

Designed by Ken Vail Graphic Design, Cambridge
Illustrations by Sean Victory
Printed in Hong Kong / China

02 01 00 99 98
10 9 8 7 6 5 4 3 2 1

ISBN 0 431 02484 7

Some words are shown in bold, **like this**. You can find out what they mean by looking in the glossary. The glossary also helps you say difficult words.

British Library Cataloguing in Publication Data

Woodhouse, Jayne
Nelson Mandela. - (Lives & times)
1. Mandela, Nelson, 1918– - Juvenile literature 2. Presidents - South Africa - Biography - Juvenile literature 3. Anti-apartheid movement - History - Juvenile literature
I. Title
968' .06'092

Acknowledgements

The Publishers would like to thank the following for permission to reproduce photographs:
The British Library Newspaper Library, with permission from The Daily Mirror, The Independent, The Pretoria News and The Star: pp21–22; Britstock – IFA: Haga p23; Chris Honeywell: p18; Link Picture Library: G English p17; Magnum Photos Ltd: I Berry p16, G Mendal p19; Rex Features: N Berman p22

Cover photograph reproduced with permission of J. Witt, Rex Features.

Our thanks to Betty Root for her comments in the preparation of this book.

Every effort has been made to contact copyright holders of any material reproduced in this book. Any omissions will be rectified in subsequent printings if notice is given to the Publisher.

Contents

The first part of this book tells you the story of Nelson Mandela.
The second part tells you how we can find out about his life.

Childhood

This is a story about a very important person. His name is Nelson Mandela. He was born in 1918 in a country called South Africa.

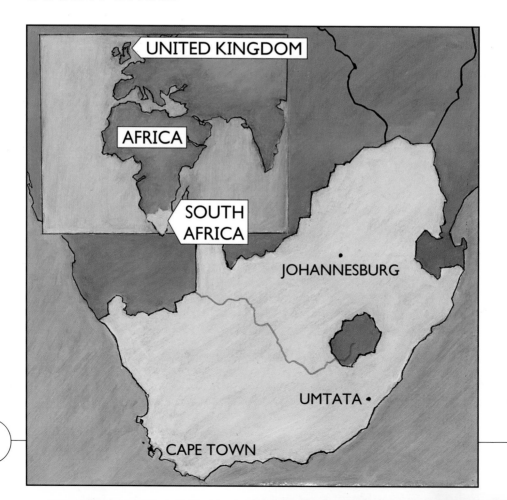

Nelson was the son of a **Thembu** chief.
His African name is Rolihlaha, which
means 'troublemaker'! Nelson grew up in
a small village. His home was made of
mud. It had a grass roof.

Growing up

When Nelson was five years old, he began
to look after the family's sheep and **calves**.
He loved to play with the other boys in
the **veld**.

Later, Nelson went to school and then to **university**. He became a **lawyer** in **Johannesburg**.

Kept apart

Both black and white people lived in South Africa. At that time white people ruled the country and made the **laws**. They kept the best houses, schools and land for themselves.

They said that all black people must live apart from white people. The South African word for this is **apartheid**. It made life very hard for black people.

Prison

'This is wrong!' Nelson and his friends said.
'This country belongs to everyone. We
must work to change the **laws**!'

The white people who ruled South Africa did not want to change the laws. In 1963, they arrested Nelson and sent him to prison. He was kept there for 27 years.

Free at last

People all over the world thought that Nelson was right. They wanted life in South Africa to change. People shouted, 'Free Nelson Mandela!' at **demonstrations**.

Not long before you were born, in 1990,
Nelson was set free. He was now 71 years
old and his hair was grey.

President

Four years later, there was an **election** in South Africa. For the first time, black people as well as white people were allowed to **vote**.

They chose Nelson Mandela to be the **president** of South Africa. The man who was a prisoner for so long had helped to change the lives of his people for ever.

Photographs

Photographs show us what Nelson looks like. This picture was taken when he was a young man, before he went to prison. In what ways does he look different now?

This photograph was taken when Nelson was set free from prison. Millions of people all around the world watched this on television, as it was happening.

Books

Nelson has written a book telling the story of his life. It is called *Long Walk to Freedom*. It tells us about his feelings and friends and what it was like in prison.

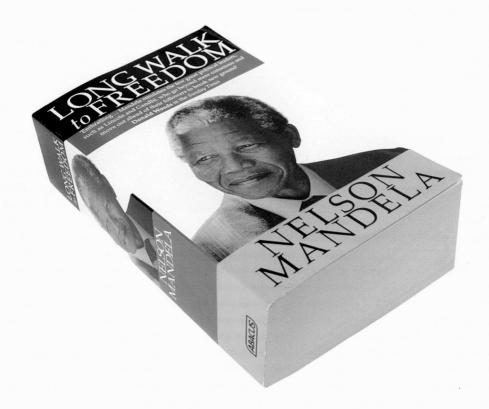

Posters

Posters still survive from the time when Nelson was in prison. They say that he should be set free.

Newspapers

We can read all about Nelson's life in the newspapers. How have the newspapers changed the way they write about him?

12,000 EYES ON NELSON

MAKING WAVES: Mandela rides with the Queen. Pictures: KENT GAVIN and ALISDAIR MACDONALD

EYE-EYE: One guardsman sneaks a look

LEADER: Prince Philip follows Mandela

Queen greets hero Mandela

By JAMES WHITAKER

ALL eyes were on Nelson Mandela yesterday as the People's Hero took London by storm.

Mandela in London: South Africans who fled from apartheid into exile can feel proud of their nation – and cry a

Grand tour: The Queen and Nelson Mandela enjoying the acclaim of the crowds outside Buckingham Palace

Photograph: Glynn Griffiths

The man who made a rainbow shine

RAYMOND WHITAKER

All around us

Some places have statues of Nelson Mandela. Streets and buildings have been named after him. Is there one near you?

Perhaps someone you know has lived in South Africa or been there on holiday. Ask them to tell you more about the events in this book.

Glossary

This glossary explains difficult words, and helps you to say words which are hard to say.

apartheid when black people and white people are kept apart. You say *a-par-tide*

autobiography a book written by someone about his or her own life

calves young cows. You say *carves*

demonstration showing your beliefs or feelings to attract attention

election when people get a chance to be chosen to be in the government

Johannesburg a very large and important city in South Africa. You say *jo-han-es-berg*

laws the rules of a country

lawyer someone who studies the rules of a country to help people who are in trouble

president the leader of a country

Thembu an African tribe or group who have lived in South Africa for hundreds of years. You say *tem-boo*

university a place to go on to for more study, after you have finished school

veld a South African word meaning open countryside. You say *velt*

vote choosing who you want to be in the government

Index